THE COMPLETE AIR FRYER COOKBOOK FOR BEGINNERS:

Healthy and Super-Easy Everyday Air Fryer Recipes.

(Basic Air Fryer Recipes)

By
Noah White

© **Copyright by Noah White 2024 - All rights reserved.**

The content contained within this book may not be reproduced, duplicated or transmitted without direct written permission from the author or the publisher. Under no circumstances will any blame or legal responsibility be held against the publisher, or author, for any damages, reparation, or monetary loss due to the information contained within this book. Either directly or indirectly. You are responsible for your own choices, actions, and results.

Legal Notice:
This book is copyright protected. This book is only for personal use. You cannot amend, distribute, sell, use, quote or paraphrase any part, or the content within this book, without the consent of the author or publisher.

Disclaimer Notice:
Please note the information contained within this document is for educational and entertainment purposes only. All effort has been executed to present accurate, up to date, and reliable, complete information. No warranties of any kind are declared or implied. Readers acknowledge that the author is not engaging in the rendering of legal, financial, medical or professional advice. The content within this book has been derived from various sources. Please consult a licensed professional before attempting any techniques outlined in this book.

By reading this document, the reader agrees that under no circumstances is the author responsible for any losses, direct or indirect, which are incurred as a result of the use of the information contained within this document, including, but not limited to, — errors, omissions, or inaccuracies.

TABLE OF CONTENTS

INTRODUCTION
5

Air Fryer Cooking Guide for Recommended Temperature & Cooking Times / 3
Bakery, Desserts & Snacks / 13
Poultry & Seafood / 14
Lamb, Pork & Beef / 15
Legumes & Vegetables / 16
Frozen Section / 18

POTATO RECIPES
21

French Fries / 22
Potato Wedges / 23
Baked Potatoes / 24
Roasted Potatoes / 25
Hasselback Potatoes / 26
Baby Potatoes / 27

Sweet Potato Crisps / 28
Baked Sweet Potato / 29
Sweet Potato Fries / 30
Baked Potatoes with Mushrooms / 31
Potatoes with Bacon / 32
Shepherd's Pie / 33

VEGETARIAN RECIPES
35

Asparagus / 36
Baked Vegetables / 37
Zucchini Fries / 38
Zucchini Patties / 39
Stuffed Zucchini / 40
Crispy Green Beans / 41
Cheesy Green Beans / 42
Fried Eggplant with Garlic / 43
Vegetable Skewers / 44

Mini Eggplant Pizza / 45
Baked Broccoli & Cauliflower / 46
Broccoli Quiche / 47
Roasted Brussels Sprouts / 48
Stuffed Bell Peppers / 49
Vegetarian Pizza / 50
Baked Mushrooms / 51
Stuffed Mushrooms / 52
Bacon Wrapped Asparagus. / 53
Tofu with Vegetables / 54

MEALS WITH EGGS
55

Egg Toast / 56
Scottish Eggs / 57
Omelette / 58
Egg Benedict / 59

Baked Egg / 60
Cheese Egg Muffins / 61
Bacon Breakfast Cups / 62

POULTRY RECIPES
63

Chicken Breasts / 64
Chicken Wings / 65
Chicken Legs / 66
Chicken Strips / 67
Chicken Thighs / 68
Whole Chicken / 69
Chicken Skewers / 70

Chicken Patties / 71
Turkey Breast / 72
Chicken with Vegetables / 73
Burritos with Chicken & Vegetables / 74
Chicken Nuggets / 75
Chicken with Broccoli / 76

MEAT RECIPES
77

Roast Beef Joint / 78
Beef Steak / 79
Rib Eye Steak / 80
Meatballs / 81
Burger Patties / 82

Crispy Bacon / 83
Sausage / 84
Lamb Chops / 85
Juicy Pork Tenderloin / 86
Pork Spare Ribs / 87

SEAFOOD RECIPES
89

Fish Sticks / 90
Scallops / 91
Salmon / 92
Cod Sticks / 93
Juicy Shrimp / 94

Tuna Steaks / 95
Salmon Patties / 96
Crispy Haddock / 97
Shrimp Skewers / 98

DESSERT RECIPES
99

Muffins / 100
Brownie / 101
Apple Crumble / 102
Lemon Cake / 103
Banana Bread / 104

Donuts / 105
Carrot Cake / 106
Peanut Butter Cookies / 107
Pineapple Upside-Down Cake / 108
Bread Pudding / 109

INTRODUCTION

Have you ever longed for the delightful crunch of fried treats but worried about the oil you're eating? If so, you're definitely not alone. Thankfully, the air fryer has emerged as a solution, allowing us to enjoy crispy foods without soaking them in oil. This fantastic device has revolutionized home cooking, letting people everywhere savour their favourite fried meals without the guilt.

A Quick Look at the History and Development of Air Fryers:

Let's dive into the intriguing development of the air fryer. While the idea of using hot air for cooking is not brand new, the air fryer as it exists today has evolved significantly. It started with a challenge: Can we enjoy crispy fried food without the unhealthy oil?

In the early 2000s, innovators in the appliance industry found the solution. They designed an appliance that mimicked the effects of deep-frying with much less oil. The air fryer was born! This kitchen miracle uses a technology that blows hot air around the food, crisping the outside while keeping the inside tender and juicy.

Since its inception, the air fryer has become essential for those who prioritize health and anyone with a busy lifestyle. It's not only praised for making healthier fried food but also for its ability to cook a variety of dishes, from snacks to desserts.

Advantages of Using Air Fryers for Healthier Meals:

Why is the air fryer considered a breakthrough in the kitchen? Here are some benefits that have made it popular among novice and experienced cooks alike.

- **Less Oil Needed:** The biggest benefit of the air fryer is that it can make food crispy with just a tiny amount of oil. Unlike traditional frying, which drowns food in oil, the air fryer coats it lightly, reducing calories and harmful fats.
- **Healthy Eating Without Losing Taste:** We all love the satisfying crunch of fried foods, but we could do without the guilt. The air fryer allows you to enjoy your favourite foods without losing the flavour or texture. It's easier to stick to your health goals when your meals are both tasty and low in oil.
- **Saves Time:** With its quick heating and cooking capabilities, the air fryer saves a lot of time. Forget waiting for oil to heat up or long baking times; this device makes cooking faster, getting you to the dining table quicker.
- **Simple Cleanup:** Another great feature of the air fryer is that it contains messes. Many parts are also dishwasher-safe, which means quicker clean-up and more time to enjoy what you've made.

Selecting the Perfect Air Fryer for Your Kitchen:

With so many air fryer models available, finding the right one might seem daunting, especially for beginners. Let's break down the selection process into manageable parts:

1. **Size and Capacity:** Air fryers vary in size, generally measured in quarts. Think about how many people you usually cook for. A small air fryer (3-4 quarts) works well for one or two people, while larger households might need a model that holds 5-6 quarts or more.
2. **Power and Temperature Flexibility:** It's essential to choose an air fryer with adjustable temperature controls and enough power (measured in watts). This gives you the ability to tailor the cooking process to different dishes.
3. **Versatility in Cooking:** Most air fryers do more than just fry; they can bake, grill, and roast as well. Think about what cooking methods you use most and pick a model that offers those features.

4. **Ease of Cleaning:** Consider air fryers with parts that are easy to remove and safe for the dishwasher. Easy cleanup makes the cooking process more enjoyable.
5. **Control Type:** Decide if you prefer manual knobs or a digital touch panel. Digital models often come with preset programs for specific foods, which can be very convenient.
6. **Brand and Reviews:** Do some research on different brands and read customer reviews. Choosing a well-respected brand with positive reviews can lead to a better and more reliable cooking experience.

By focusing on these key points, you can find an air fryer that fits your cooking style and needs. Once you have the right model, you're ready to start enjoying all the benefits of air-fried foods.

Must-Have Accessories for Your Air Fryer:

While the air fryer itself is a fantastic tool, the right accessories can truly elevate your cooking game and broaden your culinary horizons. Here are some essential accessories and tools that can enhance your air frying experience:

1. **Silicone or Parchment Liners:** Using silicone or parchment paper liners in your air fryer basket helps prevent food from sticking and simplifies cleanup. It's a small addition that makes a big difference.
2. **Grill Pan or Skewers:** To expand your cooking options, consider adding a grill pan or skewers to your setup. These are great for making grilled veggies, meats, or even kebabs, adding more versatility to your air fryer.
3. **Oil Sprayer:** An oil sprayer lets you apply a fine mist of oil, ensuring your food gets just the right amount of oil for that perfect crispy finish without excess fat.
4. **Multi-Layer Rack:** Increase your air fryer's cooking capacity with a multi-layer rack. This tool allows you to cook multiple items at once, which is a great time-saver.
5. **Tongs with Silicone Tips:** A reliable pair of tongs is crucial for safely handling hot foods. Tongs with silicone tips are gentle on non-stick surfaces, making them perfect for your air fryer basket.

6. **Meat Thermometer:** For perfectly cooked meats, a meat thermometer is indispensable. It ensures your meat is not only crispy on the outside but also perfectly done on the inside, avoiding any guesswork.

These accessories are not just additions; they're essential tools that can make your air frying simpler, more efficient, and even more fun. They allow you to explore a wider array of recipes and techniques with ease.

Tips for Effective and Safe Air Frying:

With your air fryer and essential accessories at hand, let's look at some guidelines to help you air fry efficiently and safely:

- **Preheat Your Air Fryer:** Just like a conventional oven, warming up your air fryer before use is crucial. It ensures the cooking environment is even, which helps your food cook more uniformly.
- **Avoid Overcrowding:** It might be tempting to fill the basket, but too many items can block the airflow, leading to unevenly cooked food. Make sure to leave space around each piece for the best results.
- **Flip and Shake:** To get that perfect crispiness all around, flip or shake the contents of the basket halfway through the cooking time. This step ensures that heat reaches every side of your food.
- **Light Oil Application:** A small amount of oil can greatly enhance the texture and flavor of your food. Use a brush or an oil sprayer to lightly coat your ingredients.
- **Use Cooking Spray for Sticky Foods:** For foods prone to sticking, a light spray of cooking oil on the basket or directly on the food can make a big difference.
- **Try Different Seasonings:** The air fryer is great for experimenting with flavours. Don't hesitate to try various herbs, spices, and marinades to find what best enhances your dishes.
- **Monitor Cooking Times:** Keep an eye on how your food is cooking, especially when you're still getting used to your air fryer. You might need to adjust the usual cooking times.
- **Ensure Proper Doneness:** Checking your food with a meat thermometer is important, especially for meat and poultry, to ensure they reach a safe internal temperature.
- **Prioritize Safety:** Always use the air fryer on a stable, heat-resistant surface. Follow the manufacturer's safety instructions to avoid any mishaps.

- **Ensure Good Ventilation:** Set up your air fryer in a well-ventilated area. This prevents overheating and helps the device work efficiently.

By integrating these tips into your air frying practices, you'll not only cook delicious meals but also do so safely and efficiently. In the next sections, we'll dive into a variety of recipes that cater to different tastes and dietary needs, showcasing the versatility of your air fryer. From breakfast favourites to snacks and full meals, you're sure to find recipes that will inspire you to explore new culinary possibilities with your air fryer. Let's embark on this journey of flavourful and healthy cooking!

Components and Features of an Air Fryer

Understanding the parts and functions of an air fryer can help you make the most of this versatile kitchen appliance. Here's a detailed look at its components and what they do:

PARTS:
1. **Heating Element:** Located above the food chamber, the heating element is crucial as it generates the heat needed for cooking. It quickly heats the air to a high temperature.
2. **Convection Fan:** This fan is designed to circulate the hot air around the food in the cooking chamber. It ensures that the cooking is even and speeds up the process, making your food crispy on the outside.
3. **Food Basket:** The basket holds the food as it cooks. It's designed to allow air to circulate freely around the food, ensuring it cooks evenly from all sides and achieves a crispy finish.

FUNCTIONS:
Air fryers are multifunctional, offering a range of cooking methods beyond just air frying:
1. **Air Frying:** The staple function of an air fryer uses rapid circulation of hot air to cook food evenly and quickly, resulting in a crispy exterior and moist interior. This method uses minimal oil, making it a healthier alternative to traditional frying.

2. **Baking:** Similar to an oven, the baking function uses hot air to cook sweet and savory baked goods like cakes, cookies, and muffins efficiently.
3. **Roasting:** The roasting function allows you to cook meats and vegetables by enveloping them in hot air, which helps achieve a roasted appearance and flavor with less oil.
4. **Grilling:** Some air fryers include a grilling function, which mimics the effects of grilling by using hot air to cook the food, giving it a grilled texture and flavor.
5. **Preheating:** Just like an oven, the preheat function warms the air fryer to a desired temperature before cooking, which helps enhance the texture of the food and reduces cooking time.
6. **Reheating:** This function heats cooked food without drying it out or making it soggy, which is a common issue with microwaves.
7. **Dehydrating:** Available in some models, the dehydrating function removes moisture from food such as fruits, vegetables, and meats, preserving them for longer periods.

Each of these functions adds to the air fryer's versatility, allowing you to explore a wide range of culinary tasks from a single appliance. By understanding how to utilize each feature effectively, you can enhance your cooking experience and enjoy a variety of dishes with ease.

Air Fryer Cooking Guide for Recommended Temperature & Cooking Times.

Bakery, Desserts & Snacks

BAKERY	F	C	TIME
Brownies	350	180	15-17
Cake	320	160	25
Cinnamon rolls	350	180	10
Cookies	350	180	5-6
Cupcakes	300	150	15
Hand pies	350	180	8-10
Muffins	320	160	15
Quick breads	320	160	30-35

FRUIT DESSERTS	F	C	TIME
Apple/Peach/Pear wedges coated in cinnamon sugar	350	180	10
Banana/Plantains (ripe chunks) coated in cinnamon sugar	400	200	4-5
Pineapple (chunks)	350	180	8-10
Strawberries (halved) coated with cinnamon	350	180	8

FRUIT/VEGGIE CRISPS	F	C	TIME
Apple/Banana (thinly sliced)	350	180	10
Kale (oiled & seasoned)	375	190	4-5
Beet/Sweet potato/Zucchini (thinly sliced, oiled & seasoned)	360	180	20
Will be soft after cook time, but will crisp up once they cool.			

INTRODUCTION

Poultry & Seafood

*Safe minimum internal meat temperature for chicken and turkey is 165F/75C.

CHICKEN	F	C	TIME
Breast, bone-in 1.25 lb / 550 g	370	190	25
Breast, boneless 4 oz / 110 g	380	190	12
Drumstick, 2.5 lb / 1 kg	380	190	25
Game hen, halved 2 lb / 900 g	390	200	20
Tenders, 2 lb / 900 g	400	200	10-12
Thigh, bone-in 2 lb / 900 g	380	190	22
Thigh, boneless 1.5 lb / 700 g	380	190	18-22
Whole, 6.5 lb / 2.9 kg	360	180	75
Wings, 2 lb / 900 g	400	200	16-20

TURKEY	F	C	TIME
Breast, 3 lb / 1.4 kg	360	180	40
Drumstick, 2-4 pieces	350	180	27-30
Thigh, 2 pieces bone-in	380	190	25-30

*Safe minimum internal meat temperature for duck is 165F/75C

DUCK	F	C	TIME
Whole, 5 lb / 2.3 kg	360	180	60
Breast, boneless	400	200	15-20

EGG	F	C	TIME
Hard boiled, no water required during cook	250	120	16
After cooking, submerge in cold water for 10 minutes then peel.			

*Safe minimum internal meat temperature for fish is 145F/65C

SEAFOOD	F	C	TIME
Calamari, 8 oz / 250 g	400	200	4
Fish cake	360	180	15
Fish fillet, 8 oz / 250 g	400	200	10-12
Salmon	400	200	10
Salmon fillet, 6 oz / 180 g	380	190	8-12
Salmon steaks, 8 oz / 250 g	300	150	14-18
Scallops	400	200	5-7
Shrimp	400	200	5-8
Swordfish steak	400	200	10
Tuna steak	400	200	7-10

Lamb, Pork & Beef

*Safe minimum internal meat temperature for lamb and pork is 145F/65C

LAMB	F	C	TIME
Lamb loin chops	400	200	8-12
Rack of lamb, 1.5 lb / 700 g	400	200	22

PORK	F	C	TIME
Bacon, regular streaky	400	200	5-7
Bacon, thick cut	400	200	6-10
Bratwurst sausages	350	180	15
Pork chops, bone-in 6.5 oz / 190 g	380	190	15-18
Pork chops, boneless	400	200	12-14
Pork loin, 2 lb / 900 g	400	200	55
Pork sausage	380	190	15
Pork tenderloin, 1 lb / 450 g	370	190	15

*Safe minimum internal meat temperature for beef is 145F/65C, while for meat mixtures is 160F/70C

BEEF	F	C	TIME
Burger, 4 oz / 110 g	350	180	8-12
Hotdogs	390	200	4-5
Ribeye steak, bone-in 8 oz / 220 g	400	200	10-15
Ribeye steak	400	200	8-12
Ribeye round roast, 4 lb / 1,8 kg	390	200	45-55
Filet mignon, 8 oz / 220 g	400	200	18
Flank steak, 1.5 lb / 700 g	400	200	12
Flank steak, 2 lb / 900 g	400	200	20-28
Meatballs, small	380	190	7
Meatballs, large	380	190	10
Meatloaf	370	190	30-35
Sirloin steak, 12 oz / 350 g	400	200	10-15

Legumes & Vegetables

LEGUMES	F	C	TIME
Black-eyed peas, canned to crisp	390	200	10
Chickpeas, canned to crisp	400	200	12
Edamame, fresh shelled	400	200	10
Green/snap/string beans	400	200	5-8
Green peas, canned to crisp	350	180	20
Lupins, canned to crisp	375	190	15
Peanuts, raw to oil or dry roast	320	160	10-15

SOY PRODUCTS	F	C	TIME
Tempeh	350	180	15-20
Tofu, firm or extra firm	370	190	12-15

VEGETABLES	F	C	TIME
Asparagus	400	200	5-7
Beets, chunks	380	190	8-11
Beets, whole	400	200	40
Broccoli, florets	380	190	6-10
Brussel sprouts, halved	350	175	8-12
Carrots, baby or sliced	380	190	15
Cauliflower, florets	400	200	12-15
Corn on the cob	380	190	12-16
Corn, baby	400	200	8-10
Eggplant, cubed	400	200	15
Fennel, quartered	370	190	15
Kale, oiled and seasoned	375	190	4-6
Mushrooms, sliced	400	200	5
Onions	400	200	10
Parsnips, chunks	380	190	15
Potato wedges	360	180	18-24
Potatoes, chunks or fries	400	200	12-15
Potatoes, whole baked	390	200	35-40
Potatoes, baby	400	200	15
Portabella mushrooms	350	175	12
Peppers, chunks	400	200	15
Squash, chunks	400	200	12
Sweet potato, baked	380	190	30-35
Tomatoes, cherry/vine	400	200	4-8
Zucchini, chunks	400	200	8-12

Frozen Section

When cooking packaged frozen foods from the grocery store, you can't just follow the instructions on the package. Air fryers are more intense than a regular oven.

Since they circulate heat around all the side of your food, they cook at a faster rate than traditional ovens.

A general rule of thumb for adjusting packaged frozen foods instructions:

*Reduce temperature by 50F/10C.

*Reduce the overall cook time by approximately 20%.

Let's use frozen French fries as an example. The package instructions are to cook the fries in a 450F/230C oven for 20 minutes, so you will want to set the air fryer to 400F/200C with a cook time of 16 minutes. And since you'll need to shake the basket at least once during the cooking process, you can monitor the progress and adjust the total cook time as needed.

FOOD	F	C	TIME
Bagel bites	360	180	5-6
Bread dough	380	190	15
Breaded shrimp	400	200	9
Breakfast pastry	350	180	8
Chicken nuggets, 12 oz / 350 g	380	190	10-12
Chicken tenders	380	190	12-14
Chicken wings	380	190	6-8
Corn dogs	400	200	15
Dumplings/potstickers 10 oz / 280 g	400	200	8-10
Egg rolls/spring rolls	400	200	8-10
Fish sticks, 10 oz / 280 g	400	200	8-10
French fries, thick cut	400	200	12-20
French fries, thin cut	400	200	10-14
Hash browns, 0.5 lb / 225 g	360	180	15-18
Hot pockets	370	190	11-13
Meat pie, 1-2 pcs	360	180	25
Meatballs	380	190	6-8
Mozzarella sticks, 11 oz / 310 g	350	180	4-5
Onion rings, 12 oz / 350 g	400	200	8
Pizza rolls	390	200	6-8
Potato skins	370	190	5-6
Potato wedges	350	180	25-30
Puff pastry bites, apply filling	390	200	10
Salmon fillets	360	180	8-10
Sausage rolls	400	200	15
Shoestring fries	400	200	10-15
Steak fries	380	190	22-25
Sweet potato	380	190	25-30
Tater tots	400	200	18-20
Texas toast	350	180	3-4
Veggie burger	350	180	10

This page is for your notes

French Fries

DIRECTIONS:

1. Cut potatoes into thin ¼-inch strips.
2. Add potato strips to a large mixing bowl, cover with water, and let the potatoes soak for 40 minutes. Drain the water and pat the potato strips with a paper towel.
3. Add olive oil, seasoned salt, and salt to the bowl and toss well to coat.
4. Lightly spray the air fryer basket with cooking spray.
5. Arrange potato strips into the air fryer basket in a single layer and **Air Fry** at 380 F/ 190 C for 18 minutes. Turn potato strips halfway through.
6. Serve with sauce, and enjoy.

INGREDIENTS:

- Potatoes - 4 large (1 kg), rinse & scrub
- Olive oil - 1 tbsp
- Seasoned salt - 1 tsp
- Kosher salt - 1 tsp

Cook time: 18 minutes
Serves: 6

Per Serving:
Calories 179, Carbs 10.5g,
Fat 15.6g, Protein 1.1g

Potato Wedges

DIRECTIONS:

1. In a large mixing bowl, toss potato wedges with olive oil, onion powder, garlic powder, paprika, pepper, and sea salt until well coated.
2. Transfer potato wedges into the air fryer basket and **Air Fry** for 15 minutes at 380 F/ 190 C. Shake the basket halfway through.
3. Serve potato wedges with your favorite sauce.

INGREDIENTS:

- Potatoes - 4 large (1 kg), cut into wedges
- Onion powder - ½ tsp
- Garlic powder - 1 tsp
- Paprika - 1 ½ tsp
- Olive oil - 2 tbsp
- Pepper - ½ tsp
- Sea salt - ½ tsp

Cook time: 15 minutes
Serves: 8

Per Serving:
Per Serving: Calories 368,
Carbs 36g, Fat 26g, Protein 7g

POTATO 23

Baked Potatoes

DIRECTIONS:

1. Brush potatoes with olive oil and season with pepper and salt.
2. Place potatoes into the air fryer basket and **Air Fry** for 40 minutes at 380 F/ 190 C. Turn potatoes halfway through.
3. Remove potatoes from the air fryer basket and set aside for 10 minutes.
4. Cut the potato lengthwise using a sharp knife and slightly squish the potato inside. Season with pepper and salt. Add butter and cheese to the potatoes and microwave for 30 seconds.
5. Add sour cream and a sprinkle of chives, and top with crumbled bacon.
6. Serve and enjoy.

INGREDIENTS:

- Russet potatoes – 2 (500 g), wash & using a fork, poke holes in the potatoes
- Olive oil - 1 tsp
- Pepper - to taste
- Salt - to taste
- Cheddar cheese - 4 tbsp (60 g), grated
- Chives - 1, minced
- Bacon slices - 2, cooked & crumbled
- Sour cream - 2 tbsp
- Butter - 2 tbsp

Cook time: 40 minutes
Serves: 2

Per Serving:
Calories 446, Carbs 69g, Fat 25g, Protein 12g

Roasted Potatoes

DIRECTIONS:

1. In a large bowl, toss potatoes with oil, rosemary, paprika, garlic seasoning, pepper, and salt until well coated.
2. Transfer potatoes into the air fryer basket and **Air Fry** for 25-30 minutes at 380 F/ 190 C. Shake the basket halfway through.
3. Serve and enjoy.

INGREDIENTS:

- Potatoes - 3 medium (750 g), cut into 1-inch cubes
- Rosemary - ½ tsp, crushed
- Paprika - 1 tsp
- Garlic seasoning - 1 tsp
- Olive oil - 3 tbsp
- Pepper - ½ tsp
- Salt - ½ tsp

Cook time: 25 minutes
Serves: 4

Per Serving:
Calories 295, Carbs 49.48g,
Fat 10g, Protein 5.83g

Hasselback Potatoes

DIRECTIONS:

1. Using a sharp knife, cut potatoes crosswise into 1/8-inch-thick slices, leaving about 1/4-inch of the bottom intact.
2. In a small bowl, mix butter, garlic, and Italian seasoning.
3. Brush potatoes with butter mixture and season with pepper and salt.
4. Place potatoes into the air fryer basket and **Air Fry** at 350 F/ 175 C for 15 minutes.
5. Turn potatoes and air fry for 15 minutes more.
6. Garnish with parsley and serve.

INGREDIENTS:

- Potatoes - 5 (500 g) small, wash & scrub
- Garlic cloves - 4, minced
- Italian seasoning - 1 tsp
- Butter - ½ cup (115 g), melted
- Pepper - to taste
- Salt - to taste
- Fresh parsley - minced, for garnish

Cook time: 30 minutes
Serves: 5

Per Serving:
Calories 404, Carbs 66g, Fat 18g, Protein 8g

Baby Potatoes

DIRECTIONS:

1. In a bowl, toss baby potatoes with garlic powder, olive oil, pepper, and salt.
2. Add baby potatoes into the air fryer basket and **Air Fry** for 10 minutes at 400 F/ 200 C. Stir potatoes and air fry for 3 minutes more.
3. Garnish with parsley and serve.

INGREDIENTS:

- Baby potatoes - 1 ½ lbs (680 g)
- Garlic powder - ¼ tsp
- Olive oil - 2 tbsp
- Pepper - to taste
- Salt - to taste
- Fresh parsley - minced, for garnish

Cook time: 13 minutes
Serves: 4

Per Serving:
Calories 188, Carbs 30g,
Fat 6.2g, Protein 3.6g

Sweet Potato Crisps

DIRECTIONS:

1. In a large bowl, toss sweet potato slices with garlic powder, olive oil, and salt until well coated.
2. Add sweet potato slices into the air fryer basket and **Air Fry** for 8 minutes at 350 F/ 176 C or until crisp.
3. Serve with your favorite dip and enjoy.

INGREDIENTS:

- Sweet potatoes - 2 (500 g) small, wash, scrub & slice thinly
- Garlic powder - ¼ tsp
- Olive oil - 1 tbsp
- Salt - ½ tsp

Cook time: 8 minutes
Serves: 2

Per Serving:
Calories 69, Carbs 12.6g,
Fat 6.63g, Protein 1.27g

Baked Sweet Potato

DIRECTIONS:

1. In a large bowl, toss sweet potatoes with garlic powder, olive oil, pepper, and salt until well coated.
2. Place potatoes into the air fryer basket and **Air Fry** at 390 F/ 200 C for 40 minutes or until potatoes are fork tender.
3. Remove potatoes carefully from the air fryer basket. Cut open, and top with your favorite toppings like cinnamon, brown sugar, butter, etc.

INGREDIENTS:

- Sweet potatoes - 4 (800 g) medium, wash & poke with a fork
- Garlic powder - ¼ tsp
- Olive oil - 1 tbsp
- Pepper - ¼ tsp
- Kosher salt - ¼ tsp

Cook time: 40 minutes
Serves: 4

Per Serving:
Calories 158, Carbs 27g,
Fat 3.59g, Protein 2.16g

Sweet Potato Fries

DIRECTIONS:

1. In a mixing bowl, toss sweet potato fries with olive oil.
2. Add sweet potato fries into the air fryer basket and **Air Fry** at 400 F/ 200 C for 16-18 minutes.
3. Toss sweet potato fries with spices, return them to the air fryer basket, and air fry for 4-6 minutes more.
4. Serve and enjoy.

INGREDIENTS:

- Sweet potato - 1 lb (450 g), cut into fry shape
- Garlic powder - 1 tsp
- Paprika - 1 tsp
- Olive oil - 1 tbsp
- Pepper - to taste
- Salt - to taste

Cook time: 25 minutes
Serves: 4

Per Serving:
Calories 129, Carbs 21g,
Fat 3.58g, Protein 2.73g

Baked Potatoes with Mushrooms

DIRECTIONS:

1. In a bowl, toss potatoes with half a tablespoon olive oil and season with garlic powder, pepper, and salt.
2. Add potatoes into the air fryer basket and **Air Fry** at 400 F/ 200 C for 15 minutes.
3. In a bowl, toss mushrooms with remaining olive oil, garlic powder, pepper, and salt.
4. After 15 minutes, add mushrooms to the potatoes and air fry for 10 minutes. Stir well.
5. Serve and enjoy.

INGREDIENTS:

- Potatoes – 3 (600 g), cut into large chunks
- Mushrooms - 8 oz (225 g), sliced
- Garlic powder - ¼ tsp
- Olive oil - 1 tbsp
- Pepper - to taste
- Salt - to taste

Cook time: 25 minutes
Serves: 4

Per Serving:
Calories 348, Carbs 51.72g, Fat 3.84g, Protein 7.6g

Potatoes with Bacon

DIRECTIONS:

1. In a large bowl, toss potatoes with garlic powder, olive oil, pepper, and salt.
2. Wrap each half bacon strip around each potato half and secure with a soaked toothpick.
3. Place bacon-wrapped potatoes in the air fryer basket and **Air Fry** for 15-20 minutes at 400 F/ 200 C.
4. Serve and enjoy.

INGREDIENTS:

- Baby potatoes - 1 lb (450 g), cut in half
- Bacon slices - 16, cut strips in half
- Garlic powder - ½ tsp
- Olive oil - 1 tbsp
- Pepper - to taste
- Salt - to taste

Cook time: 20 minutes
Serves: 4

Per Serving:
Calories 232, Carbs 22g,
Fat 44g, Protein 15.61g

Shepherd's Pie

DIRECTIONS:

1. For the topping: In a medium bowl, mix mashed potatoes, cheddar cheese, butter, and milk until well combined. Set aside.
2. For meat filling: Add meat, garlic, and onion in a large pan and cook over medium-high heat until meat is no longer pink. Drain excess oil.
3. Add vegetables, thyme, Worcestershire sauce, gravy mix, and 1 cup of water. Mix well, bring to a boil, and simmer over medium-high heat for 6-9 minutes or until thickened.
4. Add the meat mixture to the bottom of the heat-safe pan and top with the potato mixture.
5. Place the pan in the air fryer basket and **Bake** for 12-15 minutes at 375 F/ 190 C.
6. Serve and enjoy.

INGREDIENTS:

- Ground beef - 1 lb (450 g)
- Dried thyme - ½ tsp
- Worcestershire sauce - 2 tsp
- Brown gravy mix - 3 tbsp
- Frozen mixed vegetables - 1 cup (120 g)
- Garlic cloves - 2, minced
- Onion - 1 medium, chopped
- Mashed potatoes - 2 cups (450 g)
- Cheddar cheese - ½ cup (60 g), shredded
- Butter - 3 tbsp, melted
- Milk - ¼ cup (60 ml)

Cook time: 20 minutes
Serves: 4

Per Serving:
Calories 398, Carbs 36.3g,
Fat 76.11g, Protein 35.19g

This page is for your notes

Asparagus

DIRECTIONS:

1. Place asparagus into the air fryer basket and brush with olive oil. Sprinkle with chili flakes, black pepper, and salt. Toss to evenly coat with seasonings.
2. **Air Fry** the asparagus for 8 minutes at 375 F/ 190 C. Shake the basket halfway through.
3. Serve and enjoy.

INGREDIENTS:

- Asparagus spears, trimmed & cut the woody ends - 1 lb (450 g)
- Olive oil - 1 tbsp
- Red chili flakes, crushed - 1/4 tsp
- Black pepper - 1/4 tsp
- Salt - 1/2 tsp

Cook time: 8 minutes
Serves: 4

Per Serving:
Calories 118, Carbs 4g,
Fat 3.58g, Protein 2.53g

Baked Vegetables

DIRECTIONS:

1. In a bowl, toss cauliflower florets, zucchini, squash, onion, and bell pepper with oregano, oil, garlic, pepper, and salt.
2. Add vegetable mixture into the air fryer basket and **Air Fry** at 350 F/ 175 C for 8 minutes.
3. Stir well and air fry for 5 minutes.
4. Serve and enjoy.

INGREDIENTS:

- Cauliflower florets - 1 cup (240 g)
- Yellow squash, chopped - 1 cup (240 g)
- Red bell pepper, cut into chunks - 1/2 cup (120 g)
- Zucchini, chopped - 1 cup (240 g)
- Onions, chopped - 1/4 cup (60 g)
- Oregano - 1 tsp
- Olive oil - 1 tbsp
- Garlic, minced - 1 tsp
- Pepper - to taste
- Salt - to taste

Cook time: 13 minutes
Serves: 4

Per Serving:
Calories 116, Carbs 5.8g,
Fat 3.58g, Protein 1.39g

Zucchini Fries

DIRECTIONS:

1. Add zucchini fries into the mixing bowl and spray with olive oil spray.
2. Mix almond flour, paprika, Parmesan cheese, pepper, and salt, sprinkle over zucchini fries, and toss well to coat.
3. Add fries to the air fryer basket and **Air Fry** for 8-10 minutes at 400 F/ 200 C or until lightly golden and crispy.
4. Serve and enjoy.

INGREDIENTS:

- Zucchinis, cut into fries shape – 2 (500 g)
- Paprika - 1 tsp
- Parmesan cheese, grated - 1/4 cup (30 g)
- Almond flour - 2/3 cup (110 g)
- Pepper - to taste
- Salt - to taste
- Olive oil spray

Cook time: 10 minutes
Serves: 4

Per Serving:
Calories 116, Carbs 5.33g, Fat 2.25g, Protein 3.31g

Zucchini Patties

DIRECTIONS:

1. In a mixing bowl, add zucchini and remaining ingredients and mix until well combined.
2. Make small patties from the zucchini mixture, place them into the air fryer basket, and **Air Fry** at 375 F/ 190 C for 5 minutes.
3. Turn the patties and air fry for 7 minutes more.
4. Serve and enjoy.

INGREDIENTS:

- Egg - 1
- Zucchini, grated & squeezed – 2 (400 g)
- Onion, grated - 1/4 cup (60 g)
- Feta cheese, crumbled - 2 oz (60 g)
- Breadcrumbs - 1/4 cup (30 g)
- Flour - 1/4 cup (30 g)
- Dill, chopped - 1 tbsp
- Garlic, minced - 1 tbsp
- Chives - 2 tbsp
- Pepper - to taste
- Salt - to taste

Cook time: 12 minutes
Serves: 4

Per Serving:
Calories 67, Carbs 9.48g,
Fat 5.58g, Protein 5.7g

VEGETARIAN

Stuffed Zucchini

DIRECTIONS:

1. Scoop out the centers and discard them from each zucchini half, then place the zucchini halves on a large plate.
2. Heat oil in a pan over medium-high heat.
3. Add mushrooms and onions and sauté until onions are soft.
4. Add ground chicken and cook until browned. Add garlic, spices, tomatoes, and half the cheese and stir until well combined.
5. Evenly stuff the chicken mixture into each zucchini half, place it in the air fryer basket, and **Air Fry** at 350 F/ 175 C for 8 minutes.
6. Top with the remaining grated cheese and air fry for 2 minutes.
7. Serve and enjoy.

INGREDIENTS:

- Zucchini, halved lengthwise - 4 medium (1 kg)
- Mozzarella cheese, grated - 1 cup (120 g)
- Ground chicken - 1 lb (450 g)
- Tomatoes, diced - 1 1/2 cups (360 g)
- Garlic, minced - 1 tsp
- Paprika - 1 tbsp
- Italian seasoning - 1 tbsp
- Mushrooms, sliced - 1 cup (120 g)
- Onion, diced - 1 cup (120 g)
- Olive oil - 2 tbsp

Cook time: 20 minutes
Serves: 4

Per Serving:
Calories 250, Carbs 8g, Fat 24g, Protein 31g

Crispy Green Beans

DIRECTIONS:

1. In a shallow dish, whisk the egg and ranch dressing.
2. Mix almond flour, cheese, garlic powder, and salt in a separate shallow dish.
3. Dip each green bean in the egg mixture, then coat it with the almond flour mixture.
4. Place coated green beans into the air fryer basket and **Air Fry** for 5 minutes at 390 F/ 200 C.
5. Serve and enjoy.

INGREDIENTS:

- Egg - 1
- Green beans, trimmed - 1 lb (450 g)
- Almond flour - 1 cup (120 g)
- Parmesan cheese, grated - 1/2 cup (60 g)
- Garlic powder - 1/2 tsp
- Ranch dressing - 1 tbsp
- Garlic salt - 1/2 tsp

Cook time: 5 minutes
Serves: 6

Per Serving:
Calories 99, Carbs 5g,
Fat 5.49g, Protein 4.84g

Cheesy Green Beans

DIRECTIONS:

1. In a bowl, toss green beans with butter, cheese, garlic, pepper, and salt.
2. Transfer green beans into the air fryer basket and **Air Fry** at 370 F/ 190 C for 10 minutes.
3. Serve and enjoy.

INGREDIENTS:

- Green beans, ends snipped off - 1 lb (450 g)
- Butter, melted - 4 oz (120 g)
- Parmesan cheese, grated - 1/2 cup (60 g)
- Garlic, minced - 1 tbsp
- Pepper - to taste
- Salt - to taste

Cook time: 10 minutes
Serves: 8

Per Serving:
Calories 84, Carbs 4.93g,
Fat 13g, Protein 2.71g

Fried Eggplant with Garlic

DIRECTIONS:

1. Brush eggplant slices with oil and season with Italian seasoning, pepper, and salt.
2. Place eggplant slices into the air fryer basket and **Air Fry** for 12 minutes at 400 F/ 200 C. Turn halfway through.
3. In a small bowl, mix butter, garlic, and Parmesan cheese.
4. Brush cooked eggplant slices with the butter mixture.
5. Serve and enjoy.

INGREDIENTS:

- Eggplant, cut into 1-inch-thick slices - 1 medium (400 g)
- Garlic, minced - 1 tsp
- Butter, melted - 4 oz (60 g)
- Italian seasoning - 1 tsp
- Olive oil - 2 tbsp
- Parmesan cheese, grated - 1 tbsp
- Pepper - to taste
- Salt - to taste

Cook time: 12 minutes
Serves: 8

Per Serving:
Calories 93, Carbs 4.98g,
Fat 15.18g, Protein 1.12g

VEGETARIAN

Vegetable Skewers

DIRECTIONS:

1. Thread zucchini, bell pepper, tomatoes, onion, and mushrooms onto the soaked skewers. Season with cumin and salt.
2. Place skewers into the air fryer basket and **Air Fry** for 8 minutes at 400 F/ 200 C. Turn halfway through.
3. Serve and enjoy.

INGREDIENTS:

- Onion, cut into chunks - 1
- Red bell pepper, cut into chunks - 1/2
- Zucchini, cut into chunks - 1 small (150 g)
- Cherry tomatoes - 1 cup (150 g)
- Button mushrooms - 1 cup (150 g)
- Ground cumin - 1/2 tsp
- Salt - to taste

Cook time: 8 minutes
Serves: 6

Per Serving:
Calories 118, Carbs 8.79g, Fat 0.2g, Protein 1.4g

Mini Eggplant Pizza

DIRECTIONS:

1. Spray the air fryer basket inside with cooking spray.
2. Place the eggplant slices in the air fryer basket, brush with oil, and season with Italian seasoning, pepper, and salt.
3. **Air Fry** eggplant slices at 400 F/ 200 C for 10 minutes.
4. Place chopped tomato and basil over cooked eggplant slices and sprinkle with cheese.
5. **Air Fry** eggplant pizzas for 4 minutes.
6. Serve and enjoy.

INGREDIENTS:

- Eggplant, cut into 3/4-inch-thick slices - ½ (300 g)
- Italian herb seasoning - 1/4 tsp
- Olive oil - 1 tbsp
- Mozzarella cheese, shredded - 1/4 cup (30 g)
- Tomato, chopped - 1/4 cup (60 g)
- Fresh basil, chopped - 2 tbsp
- Pepper - to taste
- Salt - to taste

Cook time: 14 minutes
Serves: 2

Per Serving:
Calories 202, Carbs 11g, Fat 7g, Protein 6.53g

VEGETARIAN

Baked Broccoli & Cauliflower

DIRECTIONS:

1. In a mixing bowl, toss cauliflower florets and broccoli florets with red pepper flakes, olive oil, pepper, and salt.
2. Add cauliflower and broccoli mixture into the air fryer basket and **Bake** at 375 F/ 190 C for 12 minutes. Stir halfway through.
3. Sprinkle shredded cheddar cheese over cauliflower and broccoli and bake at 400 F/ 200 C for 2 minutes.
4. Serve and enjoy.

INGREDIENTS:

- Cauliflower head, cut into florets - 1 large (600 g)
- Broccoli head, cut into florets - 1 large (600 g)
- Red pepper flakes - 1 tsp
- Cheddar cheese, shredded - 2 oz (60 g)
- Olive oil - 3 tbsp
- Pepper - to taste
- Salt - to taste

Cook time: 14 minutes
Serves: 4

Per Serving:
Calories 103, Carbs 5g,
Fat 11g, Protein 3.41g

Broccoli Quiche

DIRECTIONS:

1. In a bowl, whisk eggs with milk, pepper, and salt.
2. Add cheese, tomatoes, and broccoli and stir well.
3. Pour the egg mixture into the greased air fryer baking pan.
4. Place the baking pan into the air fryer basket and **Air Fry** at 320 F/ 160 C for 8-10 minutes.
5. Slice and serve.

INGREDIENTS:

- Eggs - 2
- Broccoli florets, steamed - 1/4 cup (60 g)
- Milk - 2 tbsp
- Cheese, shredded - 1/4 cup (30 g)
- Cherry tomatoes, cut in half - 1/4 cup (60 g)
- Pepper - to taste
- Salt - to taste

Cook time: 10 minutes
Serves: 2

Per Serving:
Calories 157, Carbs 6g,
Fat 14g, Protein 13g

VEGETARIAN

Roasted Brussels Sprouts

DIRECTIONS:

1. In a bowl, toss Brussels sprouts with oil, pepper, and salt.
2. Add Brussels sprouts into the air fryer basket and **Air Fry** at 400 F/ 200 C for 10-12 minutes. Stir halfway through.
3. Serve and enjoy.

INGREDIENTS:

- Brussels sprouts, trimmed & cut in half - 1 lb (450 g)
- Olive oil - 1 tbsp
- Pepper - to taste
- Salt - to taste

Cook time: 10 minutes
Serves: 4

Per Serving:
Calories 128, Carbs 11g,
Fat 3.83g, Protein 4g

Stuffed Bell Peppers

DIRECTIONS:

1. Remove tops from bell peppers.
2. In a bowl, mix rice, beans, tomato sauce, tomatoes, parmesan cheese, and seasoning.
3. Stuff the rice mixture into the bell peppers.
4. Place stuffed pepper into air fryer basket and **Air Fry** at 360 F/ 180 C for 12 minutes.
5. Top stuffed peppers with cheese and air fry for 3 minutes or until cheese is melted.
6. Serve and enjoy.

INGREDIENTS:

- Bell peppers, remove stem & seeds - 4
- Parmesan cheese, shredded - 1 tbsp
- Mozzarella cheese, shredded - 1/2 cup (60 g)
- Italian seasoning - 1 tbsp
- Kidney beans, drained & rinsed - 14 oz (400 g)
- Cooked rice - 1 cup (200 g)
- Tomato sauce - 15 oz (425 g)
- Tomatoes, diced - 15 oz (425 g)

Cook time: 15 minutes
Serves: 4

Per Serving:
Calories 404, Carbs 30g, Fat 10g, Protein 13g

VEGETARIAN

Vegetarian Pizza

INGREDIENTS:

- Cooking spray
- Ready to bake pizza dough, 1 lb (450 g)
- Mozzarella cheese - 1/2 cup (120 g)
- Pizza sauce - 1 tbsp
- Broccoli florets - 1/4 cup (60 g)
- Mushrooms, sliced - 2
- Red bell pepper, sliced - 1
- Italian seasoning - 1/8 tsp

DIRECTIONS:

1. Lightly spray the air fryer basket with cooking spray.
2. Roll out pizza dough roughly ½-inch thick.
3. Place the rolled dough in the air fryer basket, then spread the sauce over the tortilla and top it with bell pepper, mushrooms, broccoli florets, and cheese. Sprinkle with Italian seasoning.
4. **Air Fry** pizza for 10 minutes at 400 F/ 200 C or until cheese is melted.
5. Remove the pizza from the air fryer basket.
6. Cut into pieces and serve.

Cook time: 5 minutes
Serves: 1

Per Serving:
Calories 187, Carbs 32g,
Fat 3g, Protein 23g

Baked Mushrooms

DIRECTIONS:

1. In a mixing bowl, toss mushrooms with Worcestershire sauce, onion powder, garlic powder, olive oil, and salt until well coated.
2. Add mushrooms into the air fryer basket and **Air Fry** at 400 F/ 200 C for 12-15 minutes. Stir halfway through.
3. Serve and enjoy.

INGREDIENTS:

- Mushrooms, washed, dried & sliced - 16 oz (450 g)
- Worcestershire sauce - 1 tbsp
- Onion powder - 1/4 tsp
- Garlic powder - 1/2 tsp
- Olive oil - 3 tbsp
- Salt - 3/4 tsp

Cook time: 15 minutes
Serves: 4

Per Serving:
Calories 129, Carbs 86g,
Fat 11g, Protein 10.95g

Stuffed Mushrooms

DIRECTIONS:

1. In a small bowl, mix cream cheese, sour cream, garlic powder, pepper, and salt.
2. Stuff cream cheese mixture into each mushroom cap and top each with cheddar cheese.
3. Place stuff mushrooms into the air fryer basket and **Air Fry** at 370 F/ 190 C for 8-10 minutes.
4. Serve and enjoy.

INGREDIENTS:

- Button mushrooms, cleaned & cut stems - 16 oz (450 g)
- Sour cream - 3 tbsp
- Cream cheese, softened - 6 oz (170 g)
- Garlic powder - 1/2 tsp
- Cheddar cheese, shredded - 1/4 cup (30 g)
- Pepper - to taste
- Salt - to taste

Cook time: 8 minutes
Serves: 4

Per Serving:
Calories 177, Carbs 88g,
Fat 14g, Protein 14g

Bacon Wrapped Asparagus

DIRECTIONS:

1. Season asparagus with garlic powder, pepper, and salt.
2. Wrap 3 pieces of asparagus with a slice of bacon, and repeat with the remaining asparagus and bacon.
3. Place wrapped asparagus in an air fryer basket and **Air Fry** at 390 F/ 200 C for 10 minutes. Turn the asparagus and air fry for 5 minutes more.
4. Serve and enjoy.

INGREDIENTS:

- Asparagus, trimmed & cut woody ends - 1 lb (450 g)
- Bacon slices - 8
- Garlic powder - 1/2 tsp
- Pepper - to taste
- Salt - to taste

Cook time: 15 minutes
Serves: 8

Per Serving:
Calories 89, Carbs 3g,
Fat 10g, Protein 4.63g

VEGETARIAN

Tofu with Vegetables

DIRECTIONS:

1. In a mixing bowl, whisk together rice vinegar, brown sugar, sesame oil, ginger, soy sauce, sriracha sauce, and pepper. Add tofu and mix well, then marinate for 15 minutes.
2. Add tofu into the air fryer basket and **Air Fry** at 375 F/ 190 C for 10 minutes. Shake basket.
3. Add mushrooms and broccoli, shake again, and then air fry for 12-15 minutes.
4. Serve and enjoy.

INGREDIENTS:

- Extra firm tofu, pressed & cut into 1/2-inch cubes - 1 package (450 g)
- Rice vinegar - 1 tbsp
- Brown sugar - 2 tsp
- Sesame oil - 1/2 tsp
- Fresh ginger, grated - 1 tsp
- Soy sauce - 1/2 cup (120 ml)
- Sriracha sauce - 1/2 tsp
- Broccoli head, cut into florets - 1 medium
- Mushrooms, sliced - 1/2 cup (120 g)
- Sesame seeds - 1/4 tsp
- Pepper - to taste

Cook time: 25 minutes
Serves: 4

Per Serving:
Calories 170, Carbs 13g,
Fat 13g, Protein 13.29g

MEALS WITH EGGS

Egg Toast

DIRECTIONS:

1. Use the bottom of a glass to make an indention in the bread slices.
2. Lightly spray the air fryer basket with cooking spray.
3. Place prepared bread slices into the air fryer basket.
4. Crack one egg onto each bread piece. Season with pepper and salt.
5. **Air Fry** at 340 F/ 170 C for 8 minutes or until the egg is cooked.
6. Serve and enjoy.

INGREDIENTS:

- Large eggs - 2
- Bread slices - 2
- Pepper - to taste
- Salt - to taste

Cook time: 8 minutes
Serves: 2

Per Serving:
Calories 117, Carbs 12g,
Fat 5g, Protein 4.92g

Scottish Eggs

DIRECTIONS:

1. Divide sausage into six even portions, and then flatten each portion into a patty.
2. Place one hard-boiled egg in the middle of each patty and wrap the sausage around the hard-boiled eggs. Set aside.
3. Add flour in a small bowl, beat two eggs in another small bowl, and breadcrumbs on a plate.
4. Dip each wrapped egg into the flour, then dip into the beaten egg. Roll in breadcrumbs and place on a plate.
5. Spray the air fryer basket with cooking spray.
6. Arrange eggs in the air fryer basket and **Air Fry** for 12 minutes at 390 F/ 200 C. Turn eggs halfway through.
7. Serve and enjoy.

INGREDIENTS:

- Hard-boiled eggs - 6, peeled
- Breadcrumbs - 1 cup (240 g)
- Eggs - 2, lightly beaten
- Flour - 1/3 cup (80 g)
- Pork sausage - 1 lb (450 g)

Cook time: 12 minutes
Serves: 6

Per Serving:
Calories 156, Carbs 8g,
Fat 23g, Protein 17g

Omelette

DIRECTIONS:

1. In a bowl, whisk eggs. Add onion, tomatoes, turkey slices, mushrooms, pepper, and salt, and stir well.
2. Pour the egg mixture into the greased baking pan.
3. Place baking pan into the air fryer basket and **Air Fry** for 8-10 minutes at 350 F/ 175 C.
4. Serve and enjoy.

INGREDIENTS:

- Eggs - 2
- Small onion - 1, chopped
- Grape tomatoes - 2, halved
- Turkey slices - 2, diced
- Mushrooms - 2, sliced
- Pepper - to taste
- Salt - to taste

Cook time: 8 minutes
Serves: 2

Per Serving:
Calories 153, Carbs 7g,
Fat 10g, Protein 12g

Egg Benedict

DIRECTIONS:

1. Add an inch of water to a saucepan, heat over high heat, and set a glass bowl over boiling water.
2. Add sauce ingredients to the glass bowl and whisk constantly until the sauce thickens and the temperature reaches 160 F/ 70 C. Set aside.
3. Place greased ramekins in the air fryer basket and crack one egg in each. **Air Fry** at 380 F/ 193 C for 5 minutes.
4. Place bacon slices in the air fryer basket and **Air Fry** at 400 F/ 200 C for 5 minutes.
5. While the bacon is cooking, toast the croissants.
6. To assemble, place bacon on a half muffin. Top with egg and hollandaise sauce.
7. Serve and enjoy.

INGREDIENTS:

- Eggs - 6
- Bacon slices - 15
- Butter croissant - 3

Hollandaise sauce:
- Egg yolks - 4
- Paprika - ½ tsp
- Cream - ½ cup (60g)
- Lemon juice - 1 tbsp
- Pepper - ½ tsp
- Salt - ½ tsp

Cook time: 20 minutes
Serves: 6

Per Serving:
Calories 202, Carbs 16g,
Fat 42g, Protein 22g

Baked Egg

DIRECTIONS:

1. Grease the ramekin with cooking spray.
2. Add egg, spinach, milk, bacon, and cheese to the ramekin. Season with pepper and salt. Stir gently.
3. Place the ramekin in an air fryer basket and **Air Fry** at 330 F/ 165 C for about 10 minutes.
4. Serve and enjoy.

INGREDIENTS:

- Large egg - 1
- Parmesan cheese - 2 tsp, grated
- Frozen spinach - 1 tbsp, thawed
- Bacon slice - 1, cooked & chopped
- Milk - 1 tbsp
- Pepper - to taste
- Salt - to taste

Cook time: 10 minutes
Serves: 1

Per Serving:
Calories 117, Carbs 6g, Fat 16g, Protein 8g

Cheese Egg Muffins

DIRECTIONS:

1. In a bowl, whisk together the eggs, bacon, milk, cheese, pepper, and salt until well combined.
2. Pour egg mixture into silicone muffin molds, place in an air fryer basket, and **Air Fry** for 6 minutes at 350 F/ 175 C or until the eggs are set.
3. Serve and enjoy.

INGREDIENTS:

- Large eggs - 6
- Bacon slices - 2, cooked & crumbled
- Milk - 2 tbsp
- Cheddar cheese - ¼ cup (30 g), shredded
- Pepper - to taste
- Salt - to taste

Cook time: 6 minutes
Serves: 4

Per Serving:
Calories 41, Carbs 0.7g,
Fat 3.47g, Protein 1.75g

Bacon Breakfast Cups

DIRECTIONS:

1. Line 8 silicone muffin mold with 1 slice of bacon each.
2. Crack an egg into each mold, season with pepper and salt, and give each cup a sprinkle of cheese.
3. Place muffin molds into the air fryer basket and **Air Fry** at 330 F/ 165 C for 10 minutes.
4. Serve and enjoy.

INGREDIENTS:

- Eggs - 8
- Cheddar cheese - 1 cup (120 g), shredded
- Bacon slices - 8
- Pepper - to taste
- Salt - to taste

Cook time: 10 minutes
Serves: 8

Per Serving:
Calories 295, Carbs 1.95g, Fat 24g, Protein 15g

POULTRY RECIPES

Chicken Breasts

DIRECTIONS:

1. In a small bowl, mix butter, smoked paprika, garlic powder, black pepper, and salt.
2. Brush chicken breasts with butter mixture.
3. Place chicken breasts into the air fryer basket and **Air Fry** at 350 F/ 175 C for 15 minutes.
4. Turn chicken breasts and air fry for 5 minutes more or until the internal temperature of the chicken reaches 165 F/ 75 C.
5. Serve and enjoy.

INGREDIENTS:

- Chicken breasts, boneless & skinless – 4 (600 g)
- Garlic powder - 1/4 tsp
- Butter, melted - 2 tbsp
- Black pepper - 1/4 tsp
- Smoked paprika - 1/4 tsp
- Salt - 1/2 tsp

Cook time: 20 minutes
Serves: 4

Per Serving:
Calories 551, Carbs 0.34g,
Fat 32g, Protein 60g

Chicken Wings

DIRECTIONS:

1. In a mixing bowl, toss chicken wings with butter, garlic powder, smoked paprika, brown sugar, black pepper, chili powder, and salt until well coated.
2. Add chicken wings into the air fryer basket and **Air Fry** at 350 F/ 175 C for 15 minutes.
3. Turn chicken wings and **Air Fry** at 400 F/ 200 C for 15 minutes more.
4. Serve and enjoy.

INGREDIENTS:

- Chicken wings - 2 lbs (900 g)
- Brown sugar - 1 tbsp
- Chili powder - 1 tbsp
- Butter, melted - 1/4 cup
- Smoked paprika - 1 tsp
- Garlic powder - 1 tsp
- Black pepper - 1 tsp
- Salt - 1 tsp

Cook time: 30 minutes
Serves: 8

Per Serving:
Calories 200, Carbs 1.17g,
Fat 9.75g, Protein 25.19g

Chicken Legs

DIRECTIONS:

1. In a bowl, toss chicken legs with Creole seasoning, oil, and salt.
2. Add chicken legs into the air fryer basket and **Air Fry** for 15-20 minutes at 400 F/ 200 C. Turn halfway through.
3. Serve and enjoy.

INGREDIENTS:

- Chicken legs - 6
- Creole seasoning - 1 tbsp
- Olive oil - 1 tbsp
- Salt - to taste

Cook time: 20 minutes
Serves: 6

Per Serving:
Calories 343, Carbs 0.83g,
Fat 13.43g, Protein 50.84g

Chicken Strips

DIRECTIONS:

1. In a bowl, mix buttermilk, black pepper, hot sauce, and salt. Add chicken strips and mix well, cover, and place in refrigerator for 2 hours.
2. In a shallow dish, mix breadcrumbs, oil, and cayenne pepper.
3. Remove chicken strips from marinade and coat with breadcrumb mixture.
4. Place chicken strips into the air fryer basket and **Air Fry** at 350 F/ 175 C for 12 minutes.
5. Serve and enjoy.

INGREDIENTS:

- Chicken breasts, boneless & cut into 3/4-inch strips - 1/2 lb (225 g)
- Breadcrumbs - 6 tbsp
- Black pepper - 1/8 tsp
- Hot pepper sauce - 3/4 tbsp
- Buttermilk - 1/2 cup (120 ml)
- Olive oil - 1/2 tbsp
- Cayenne pepper - 1/8 tsp
- Salt - 1/2 tsp

Cook time: 12 minutes
Serves: 4

Per Serving:
Calories 126, Carbs 1.11g, Fat 7.88g, Protein 12.37g

Chicken Thighs

DIRECTIONS:

1. In a small bowl, mix garlic powder, ground ginger, paprika, pepper, and salt.
2. Rub chicken thighs with spice mixture, place into the air fryer basket, and **Air Fry** at 400 F/ 200 C for 10 minutes.
3. Flip the chicken and air fry for 5 minutes more.
4. Serve and enjoy.

INGREDIENTS:

- Chicken thighs, bone-in - 4
- Garlic powder - 2 tsp
- Ground ginger - 1/4 tsp
- Paprika - 2 tsp
- Pepper - to taste
- Salt - to taste

Cook time: 15 minutes
Serves: 4

Per Serving:
Calories 440, Carbs 3g,
Fat 32g, Protein 32g

Whole Chicken

DIRECTIONS:

1. In a small bowl, mix onion powder, oregano, basil, black pepper, paprika, and salt.
2. Rub spice mixture all over the chicken. Place the chicken in an air fryer basket and **Air Fry** for 60 minutes at 360 F/ 180 C. Flip halfway through.
3. Slice and serve.

INGREDIENTS:

- Whole chicken, remove giblets - 4 lbs (1.8 kg)
- Dried oregano - 1 tsp
- Dried basil - 1 tsp
- Onion powder - 1/2 tsp
- Ground black pepper - 1/2 tsp
- Paprika - 1 tsp
- Salt - 1 1/2 tsp

Cook time: 60 minutes
Serves: 6

Per Serving:
Calories 621, Carbs 60g,
Fat 21g, Protein 49g

Chicken Skewers

DIRECTIONS:

1. Add chicken, bell pepper, and remaining ingredients into the mixing bowl and mix well. Cover and place in the refrigerator for 2 hours.
2. Thread marinated chicken and red bell pepper onto the soaked skewers.
3. Place skewers into the air fryer basket and **Air Fry** at 380 F/ 190 C for 16 minutes. Turn halfway through.
4. Serve and enjoy.

INGREDIENTS:

- Chicken breasts, boneless & cut into chunks – 2 (300 g)
- Red bell pepper, cut into 1-inch pieces - 1
- Oregano - 1 tsp
- Red wine vinegar - 2 tbsp
- Olive oil - 1/4 cup (60 ml)
- Lemon juice - 1
- Garlic clove, minced - 1
- Pepper - to taste
- Salt - to taste

Cook time: 16 minutes
Serves: 6

Per Serving:
Calories 256, Carbs 2.26g, Fat 18g, Protein 20.59g

Chicken Patties

DIRECTIONS:

1. In a bowl, mix chicken with remaining ingredients until well combined.
2. Make equal shapes of patties from the chicken mixture, place them into the air fryer basket, and **Air Fry** at 360 F/ 180 C for 10 minutes or until cooked.
3. Serve and enjoy.

INGREDIENTS:

- Egg - 1
- Ground chicken - 1/2 lb (225 g)
- Poultry seasoning - 2 tsp
- Breadcrumbs - 1/2 cup (120 g)
- Pepper - to taste
- Salt - to taste

Cook time: 10 minutes
Serves: 2

Per Serving:
Calories 241, Carbs 3.67g, Fat 14g, Protein 24.14g

Turkey Breast

DIRECTIONS:

1. In a small bowl, mix butter, pepper, thyme, sage, and salt and rub all over the turkey breast.
2. Place turkey breast into the air fryer basket and **Air Fry** at 325 F/ 160 C for 30 minutes.
3. Turn the turkey breast and air fry for 30 minutes more or until the internal temperature of the turkey breast reaches 165 F/ 75 C.
4. Slice and serve.

INGREDIENTS:

- Turkey breast, bone-in & skin-on - 2 lbs (900 g)
- Butter - 1 tbsp
- Fresh sage, chopped - 1/2 tsp
- Fresh thyme, chopped - 1/2 tsp
- Pepper - 1/4 tsp
- Salt - 1 tsp

Cook time: 60 minutes
Serves: 8

Per Serving:
Calories 192, Carbs 0.18g, Fat 9.23g, Protein 24.78g

Chicken with Vegetables

DIRECTIONS:

1. In a mixing bowl, toss the chicken with the remaining ingredients.
2. Add chicken mixture into the air fryer basket and **Air Fry** for 12-15 minutes at 400 F/ 200 C. Stir halfway through.
3. Serve and enjoy.

INGREDIENTS:

- Chicken breasts, boneless & cut into pieces – 2 (300 g)
- Onion, sliced - 1 small
- Red bell pepper, sliced - 1
- Yellow bell pepper, sliced - 1
- Green bell pepper, sliced - 1
- Olive oil - 2 tbsp
- Soy sauce - 1/4 cup (60 ml)
- Garlic powder - 1 tbsp
- Ground ginger - 1/2 tsp
- Pepper - to taste
- Salt - to taste

Cook time: 15 minutes
Serves: 4

Per Serving:
Calories 389, Carbs 11g, Fat 23g, Protein 32g

Burritos with Chicken & Vegetables

DIRECTIONS:

1. Add all Burrito mixture into a large bowl and stir to combine.
2. Divide rice equally onto tortillas.
3. Equally, divide the burrito mixture on the tortillas.
4. Top each tortilla with mozzarella cheese and roll into burritos.
5. Place burritos into the air fryer basket and **Air Fry** at 340 F/ 170 C for 5 minutes.
6. Serve and enjoy.

INGREDIENTS:

Burrito Mixture:
- Chicken breast, cooked & shredded - 2 ½ cups (500 g)
- Black beans, drained & rinsed - 2 cans (800 g)
- Salsa - 1/4 cup (60 g)
- Lime juice - 2 tbsp
- Fresh cilantro, chopped - 1/2 cup (25 g)
- Green onions, diced - 3
- Tomato, diced - 1 cup (200 g)

Burritos:
- Tortillas, medium - 12
- Mozzarella cheese, shredded - 1 cup (120 g)
- Cooked rice - 2 cups (450 g)

Cook time: 5 minutes
Serves: 12

Per Serving:
Calories 265, Carbs 42.91g, Fat 8.72g, Protein 11.42g

Chicken Nuggets

DIRECTIONS:

1. In a shallow dish, mix flour and chicken seasoning.
2. In a separate shallow dish, add ranch dressing.
3. In a third shallow dish, mix breadcrumbs and shredded cheese.
4. Coat chicken pieces with flour, dip them in ranch dressing, and finally, coat them with the cheese mixture.
5. Place coated chicken pieces in an air fryer basket and **Air Fry** at 325 F/ 160 C for 10 minutes.
6. Turn on the chicken tenders and air fry for 15 minutes more.
7. Serve and enjoy.

INGREDIENTS:

- Chicken breast, boneless, skinless & cut into pieces - 14 oz (400 g)
- Ranch dressing - 1/3 cup (80 ml)
- Chicken seasoning - 2 tsp
- Cheddar cheese, shredded - 1/2 cup (60 g)
- Breadcrumbs - 2/3 cup (70 g)
- All-purpose flour - 2 tbsp

Cook time: 25 minutes
Serves: 8

Per Serving:
Calories 399, Carbs 2.1g,
Fat 15.67g, Protein 59.31g

Chicken with Broccoli

DIRECTIONS:

1. In a mixing bowl, add chicken, broccoli florets, and remaining ingredients and mix well.
2. Add the chicken and broccoli mixture into the air fryer basket and **Air Fry** at 380 F/ 190 C for 15-20 minutes. Stir 2-3 times.
3. Serve and enjoy.

INGREDIENTS:

- Chicken breasts, boneless & cut into 1-inch pieces - 1 lb (450 g)
- Broccoli florets - 2 cups (150 g)
- Soy sauce - 1 tbsp
- Garlic powder - 1 tsp
- Olive oil - 3 tbsp
- Hot sauce - 2 tsp
- Rice vinegar - 2 tsp
- Sesame oil - 1 tsp
- Pepper - to taste
- Salt - to taste

Cook time: 20 minutes
Serves: 4

Per Serving:
Calories 318, Carbs 3.4g, Fat 22.75g, Protein 24.47g

MEAT RECIPES

Roast Beef Joint

DIRECTIONS:

1. In a small bowl, mix garlic powder, thyme, oregano, onion powder, parsley, pepper, and salt.
2. Brush the beef roast with oil and rub it with the spice mixture.
3. Place the beef roast into the air fryer basket and Roast at 390 F/ 200 C for 15 minutes.
4. Turn the heat to 360 F/ 180 C and **Roast** for 20 minutes more.
5. Slice and serve.

INGREDIENTS:

- Beef roast - 2 lbs (900 g)
- Parsley - 2 tsp
- Onion powder - 2 tsp
- Garlic powder - 2 tsp
- Olive oil - 1 tbsp
- Oregano - 2 tsp
- Thyme - 2 tsp
- Pepper - to taste
- Salt - to taste

Cook time: 35 minutes
Serves: 4

Per Serving:
Calories 461, Carbs 3.62g,
Fat 22g, Protein 61g

Beef Steak

DIRECTIONS:

1. In a small bowl, mix melted butter, garlic, pepper, and salt.
2. Brush the steaks with butter mixture and place them into the air fryer basket. **Air Fry** at 400 F/ 200 C for 7 minutes.
3. Slice and serve.

INGREDIENTS:

- Steak - 10 oz (280 g)
- Butter, melted - 2 tbsp
- Garlic cloves, minced - 1 tbsp
- Pepper - to taste
- Salt - to taste

Cook time: 7 minutes
Serves: 2

Per Serving:
Calories 183, Carbs 3.4g,
Fat 25.6g, Protein 40.2g

Rib Eye Steak

DIRECTIONS:

1. Rub the steak with seasoning, place it into the air fryer basket, and **Air Fry** for 10 minutes at 400 F/ 200 C.
2. Serve and enjoy.

INGREDIENTS:

- Rib-eye steak - 8 oz (225 g)
- Steak seasoning - 1 tbsp

Cook time: 10 minutes
Serves: 2

Per Serving:
Calories 226, Carbs 4.48g, Fat 12g, Protein 22.21g

Meatballs

DIRECTIONS:

1. In a mixing bowl, mix meat and remaining ingredients until well combined.
2. Make small balls from the meat mixture, place them into the air fryer basket, and **Air Fry** for 12 minutes at 400 F/ 200 C. Turn halfway through.
3. Serve and enjoy.

INGREDIENTS:

- Egg - 1
- Ground beef - 1 lb (450 g)
- Ground pork - 1/2 lb (225 g)
- Parsley, chopped - 2 tbsp
- Milk - 2 tbsp
- Breadcrumbs - 1/3 cup (40 g)
- Onion powder - 1/2 tsp
- Italian seasoning - 1/2 tsp
- Parmesan cheese, grated - 1 tbsp
- Pepper - to taste
- Salt - to taste

Cook time: 12 minutes
Serves: 16

Per Serving:
Calories 126, Carbs 0.6g,
Fat 8g, Protein 11.22g

Burger Patties

DIRECTIONS:

1. Add ground beef and remaining ingredients into the mixing bowl and mix until well combined.
2. Make equal shapes of patties from the meat mixture.
3. Place patties into the air fryer basket and **Air Fry** at 400 F/ 200 C for 15 minutes. Turn halfway through.
4. Serve and enjoy.

INGREDIENTS:

- Ground beef - 1 lb (450 g)
- Onion, chopped - 1/2 cup (75 g)
- Olives, pitted & chopped - 1/4 cup (37 g)
- Feta cheese, crumbled - 3/4 cup (112 g)
- Garlic powder - 1/4 tsp
- Steak seasoning - 1/2 tsp
- Worcestershire sauce - 2 tbsp
- Salt - to taste

Cook time: 15 minutes
Serves: 4

Per Serving:
Calories 386, Carbs 5g,
Fat 25g, Protein 32.25g

Crispy Bacon

DIRECTIONS:

1. Arrange bacon slices in an air fryer basket.
2. **Air Fry** bacon slices at 350 F/ 175 C for 12-15 minutes or until crispy.
3. Serve and enjoy.

INGREDIENTS:

- Bacon slices - 8

Cook time: 12 minutes
Serves: 8

Per Serving:
Calories 106, Carbs 0.22g,
Fat 10g, Protein 3.26g

Sausage

DIRECTIONS:

1. Arrange sausage in an air fryer basket and **Air Fry** for 14 minutes at 370 F/ 185 C.
2. Turn sausages halfway through.
3. Serve and enjoy.

INGREDIENTS:

- Sausage links - 4

Cook time: 14 minutes
Serves: 4

Per Serving:
Calories 125, Carbs 1.76g,
Fat 7g, Protein 13.56g

Lamb Chops

DIRECTIONS:

1. Add lamb chops and remaining ingredients into the zip-lock bag. Seal the bag and place it in the refrigerator for 30 minutes.
2. Place marinated lamb chops into the air fryer basket and **Air Fry** at 400 F/ 200 C for 12 minutes. Turn halfway through.
3. Serve and enjoy.

INGREDIENTS:

- Lamb chops - 4
- Lime zest - 1 tsp
- Fresh lemon juice - 4 tbsp (60 ml)
- Garlic powder - 3/4 tsp
- Chili powder - 1/4 tsp
- Fresh mint, chopped - 1 tbsp
- Honey - 2 tbsp
- Olive oil - 2 tbsp
- Balsamic vinegar - 1 tbsp
- Pepper - to taste
- Salt - to taste

Cook time: 12 minutes
Serves: 4

Per Serving:
Calories 247, Carbs 12g,
Fat 14.34g, Protein 18.3g

Juicy Pork Tenderloin

DIRECTIONS:

1. Add pork tenderloin and remaining ingredients into the zip-lock bag. Seal the bag and place it in the refrigerator overnight.
2. Place marinated pork tenderloin into the air fryer basket and **Air Fry** at 350 F/ 175 C for 25 minutes. Turn pork tenderloin after 15 minutes.
3. Slice and serve.

INGREDIENTS:

- Pork tenderloin - 1 1/2 lbs (675 g)
- Garlic cloves, minced - 2
- Fennel seeds, crushed - 1/4 tsp
- Olive oil - 1 tbsp
- Dried thyme - 1 tsp
- Pepper - to taste
- Salt - to taste

Cook time: 25 minutes
Serves: 4

Per Serving:
Calories 280, Carbs 1.67g, Fat 9.4g, Protein 44.86g

Pork Spare Ribs

DIRECTIONS:

1. Add meat and remaining ingredients into the zip-lock bag. Seal the bag and place it in the refrigerator overnight.
2. Remove meat from the marinade, place it into the air fryer basket, and **Air Fry** at 375 F/ 190 C for 10 minutes.
3. Serve and enjoy.

INGREDIENTS:

- Spare ribs, cut into small pieces - 1 1/2 lbs (675 g)
- Ginger, minced - 1 tsp
- Garlic, minced - 1 tsp
- Sesame oil - 1 tbsp
- Honey - 1 tbsp
- Soy sauce - 1 tbsp
- Wine - 1 tbsp
- Black bean paste - 1 tbsp

Cook time: 10 minutes
Serves: 4

Per Serving:
Calories 299, Carbs 5.97g,
Fat 13g, Protein 35g

This page is for your notes

SEAFOOD RECIPES

Fish Sticks

DIRECTIONS:

1. In a small bowl, whisk the egg.
2. In a shallow bowl, add flour.
3. In a separate shallow bowl, mix breadcrumbs, lemon pepper seasoning, paprika, and salt.
4. Coat each fish strip with flour, then dip it in egg, and finally coat it with breadcrumb mixture.
5. Place the coated fish strips into the air fryer basket and **Air Fry** at 400 F/ 200 C for 10 minutes.
6. Serve and enjoy.

INGREDIENTS:

- Egg, lightly beaten - 1
- Cod fillets, cut into 1-inch strips - 1 lb (450 g)
- Lemon pepper seasoning - 1/2 tsp
- Paprika - 1/2 tsp
- Breadcrumbs - 1/2 cup (60 g)
- All-purpose flour - 1/2 cup (60 g)
- Salt - 1/2 tsp

Cook time: 10 minutes
Serves: 4

Per Serving:
Calories 168, Carbs 12.3g, Fat 3.4g, Protein 21.9g

Scallops

DIRECTIONS:

1. In a bowl, toss scallops with oil, lemon juice, garlic, butter, pepper, and salt.
2. Add scallops into the air fryer basket and **Air Fry** at 400 F/ 200 C for 6-8 minutes. Stir halfway through.
3. Serve and enjoy.

INGREDIENTS:

- Scallops - 1 lb (450 g)
- Garlic, minced - 1 tbsp
- Olive oil - 1 tbsp
- Lemon juice - 1 lemon
- Butter, melted - 2 tbsp
- Pepper - to taste
- Salt - to taste

Cook time: 8 minutes
Serves: 4

Per Serving:
Calories 169, Carbs 6.17g,
Fat 9.49g, Protein 14.88g

Salmon

DIRECTIONS:

1. Place ground peppercorns in a dish.
2. In a small bowl, mix butter, thyme, lemon juice, and garlic.
3. Brush salmon fillets with butter mixture and coat with ground peppercorns.
4. Place salmon fillets into the air fryer basket and **Air Fry** for 7 minutes at 400 F/ 200 C.
5. Serve and enjoy.

INGREDIENTS:

- Salmon fillets – 4 (680 g)
- Garlic cloves, chopped - 2
- Lemon juice - 2 tbsp
- Butter, melted - 2 tbsp
- Ground peppercorns - 3 tbsp
- Dried thyme - 1/4 tsp

Cook time: 7 minutes
Serves: 4

Per Serving:
Calories 367, Carbs 0.83g, Fat 15g, Protein 52g

Cod Sticks

DIRECTIONS:

1. In a small bowl, add milk.
2. In a shallow dish, mix cornmeal, garlic powder, onion powder, flour, cheese, basil, pepper, and salt.
3. Dip each fish piece in milk, and then coat it with the cornmeal mixture.
4. Place coated fish pieces into the air fryer basket and **Air Fry** at 400 F/ 200 C for 14 minutes. Turn halfway through.
5. Serve and enjoy.

INGREDIENTS:

- Cod fillets, cut into equal pieces - 1 lb (450 g)
- Dried basil - 1/2 tsp
- Parmesan cheese, grated - 1 tbsp
- Flour - 2 tbsp
- Ground cornmeal - 1/4 cup (45 g)
- Milk - 1/3 cup (80 ml)
- Onion powder - 1/8 tsp
- Garlic powder - 1/8 tsp
- Pepper - to taste
- Salt - to taste

Cook time: 14 minutes
Serves: 4

Per Serving:
Calories 152, Carbs 13g,
Fat 1.71g, Protein 19g

Juicy Shrimp

DIRECTIONS:

1. In a bowl, toss shrimp with paprika, garlic powder, oil, Italian seasoning, pepper, and salt until well coated.
2. Add shrimp into the air fryer basket and **Air Fry** at 400 F/ 200 C for 8 minutes.
3. Serve and enjoy.

INGREDIENTS:

- Shrimp, peeled & deveined - 1 lb (450 g)
- Olive oil - 2 tsp
- Garlic powder - 1/2 tsp
- Italian seasoning - 1/2 tsp
- Paprika - 1/4 tsp
- Pepper - to taste
- Salt - to taste

Cook time: 8 minutes
Serves: 4

Per Serving:
Calories 141, Carbs 1.64g,
Fat 3.84g, Protein 23.48g

Tuna Steaks

DIRECTIONS:

1. In a bowl, mix tuna steak, honey, vinegar, oil, ginger, and soy sauce. Cover and place in refrigerator for 30 minutes.
2. Remove tuna steaks from the marinade, place them into the air fryer basket, and **Air Fry** at 380 F/ 190 C for 4 minutes.
3. Serve and enjoy.

INGREDIENTS:

- Tuna steaks, boneless – 2 (450 g)
- Ginger, grated - 1 tsp
- Honey - 2 tsp
- Rice vinegar - 1/2 tsp
- Sesame oil - 1 tsp
- Soy sauce - 1/4 cup (60 ml)

Cook time: 4 minutes
Serves: 2

Per Serving:
Calories 517, Carbs 13g,
Fat 28g, Protein 48.78g

Salmon Patties

DIRECTIONS:

1. In a bowl, mix salmon, egg, coriander, smoked paprika, green onion, and salt until well combined.
2. Make patties from the salmon mixture, place them into the air fryer basket, and **Air Fry** for 8 minutes at 360 F/ 180 C. Turn halfway through.
3. Serve and enjoy.

INGREDIENTS:

- Egg - 1
- Salmon, drained & minced - 14 oz can (400 g)
- Fresh coriander, chopped - 1/4 cup (15 g)
- Smoked paprika - 1 tsp
- Green onion, minced - 1/4 cup (15 g)
- Salt - to taste

Cook time: 8 minutes
Serves: 6

Per Serving:
Calories 125, Carbs 0.57g, Fat 6.42g, Protein 15g

Crispy Haddock

DIRECTIONS:

1. In a shallow dish, whisk egg whites.
2. Add flour to a plate. In a separate shallow dish, mix breadcrumbs, pepper, lemon pepper seasoning, and salt.
3. Coat the haddock with flour, dip it in egg, and finally coat it with breadcrumbs.
4. Place the coated haddock into the air fryer basket and **Air Fry** for 12 minutes at 350 F/ 175 C.
5. Serve and enjoy.

INGREDIENTS:

- Egg whites - 2
- Haddock fish - 8 oz (225 g)
- Lemon pepper seasoning - 2 tsp
- Breadcrumbs - 1/3 cup (40 g)
- Flour - 1/4 cup (30 g)
- Pepper - to taste
- Salt - to taste

Cook time: 12 minutes
Serves: 2

Per Serving:
Calories 215, Carbs 14g,
Fat 1.34g, Protein 34.27g

Shrimp Skewers

DIRECTIONS:

1. In a bowl, mix shrimp, cumin, paprika, garlic paste, cilantro, lemon juice, pepper, and salt.
2. Thread shrimp onto the skewers.
3. Place shrimp skewers into the air fryer basket and **Air Fry** for 5-8 minutes at 350 F/ 175 C. Turn halfway through.
4. Serve and enjoy.

INGREDIENTS:

- Shrimp, peeled & deveined - 1/2 lb (225 g)
- Paprika - 1/2 tsp
- Garlic paste - 1/2 tsp
- Cilantro, chopped - 1 tbsp
- Lemon juice - 1 lemon
- Ground cumin - 1/2 tsp
- Pepper - to taste
- Salt - to taste

Cook time: 8 minutes
Serves: 4

Per Serving:
Calories 66, Carbs 2.86g,
Fat 0.81g, Protein 11.35g

DESSERT RECIPES

Muffins

INGREDIENTS:

- Egg - 1
- Blueberries - 1/2 cup (120 g)
- Flour - 2/3 cup (85 g)
- Baking powder - 1/2 tsp
- Olive oil - 1/3 cup (80 ml)
- Sugar - 1/3 cup (65 g)
- Lemon zest - 1 tsp
- Vanilla - 1/4 tsp
- Water - 2 tbsp
- Salt - Pinch

DIRECTIONS:

1. In a bowl, whisk the egg with vanilla, oil, sugar, water, and lemon zest.
2. In a separate bowl, mix flour, baking powder, and salt.
3. Add flour mixture into the egg mixture and mix until well combined. Add blueberries and fold well.
4. Divide the batter into the silicone muffin molds.
5. Place muffin molds into the air fryer basket and **Bake** at 350 F/ 175 C for 15-17 minutes.
6. Serve and enjoy.

Cook time: 17 minutes
Serves: 3

Per Serving:
Calories 438, Carbs 42g, Fat 27g, Protein 6.16g

Brownie

DIRECTIONS:

1. Add all ingredients except walnuts and chocolate chips into the mixing bowl and mix until well combined.
2. Add walnuts and chocolate chips and fold well.
3. Pour batter into the greased air fryer cake pan.
4. Place the cake pan into the air fryer basket and **Air Fry** at 350 F/ 175 C for 8 minutes.
5. Slice and serve.

INGREDIENTS:

- Almond flour - 1 1/2 cups (180 g)
- Vanilla - 1 tsp
- Butter, melted - 3 tbsp
- Banana, mashed - 1
- Walnuts, chopped - 1/4 cup (30 g)
- Chocolate chips - 1/4 cup (45 g)
- Baking soda - 1/2 tsp
- Chocolate whey protein powder - 1/3 cup (40 g)
- Salt - 1/4 tsp

Cook time: 8 minutes
Serves: 6

Per Serving:
Calories 99, Carbs 4.25g,
Fat 9g, Protein 0.8g

Apple Crumble

DIRECTIONS:

1. In a bowl, mix flour, butter, and sugar until crumbly. Stir in baking powder, nutmeg, and cinnamon.
2. Divide some crumble mixture into the two greased ramekins and top with apples. Top with remaining crumble.
3. Cover ramekins with foil, place them into the air fryer basket, and **Air Fry** for 15-20 minutes at 350 F/ 175 C.
4. Remove foil and cook for 2 minutes more.
5. Serve and enjoy.

INGREDIENTS:

- Apples, peeled, cored & chopped - 2 1/2 cups (320 g)
- Butter, cubed - 1/4 cup (56 g)
- Sugar - 1/2 cup (100 g)
- All-purpose flour - 1 cup (120 g)
- Nutmeg - 1/4 tsp
- Baking powder - 1/2 tsp
- Cinnamon - 1/2 tsp

Cook time: 20 minutes
Serves: 2

Per Serving:
Calories 254, Carbs 92g, Fat 24.12g, Protein 7.7g

Lemon Cake

DIRECTIONS:

1. Beat eggs in a large mixing bowl.
2. Add oil, pudding mix, water, and cake mix and stir until well combined.
3. Pour batter into the greased baking pan.
4. Place baking pan in air fryer basket and **Bake** at 350 F/ 175 C for 35 minutes.
5. For syrup: Add all syrup ingredients into the bowl and mix until well combined.
6. Once the cake is done, poke holes all over the cake using a fork, then pour syrup over the cake and let it cool completely.
7. Slice and serve.

INGREDIENTS:

- Eggs - 4
- Cake mix - 15.25 oz (430 g)
- Olive oil - 3/4 cup (180 ml)
- Water - 3/4 cup (180 ml)
- Instant lemon pudding mix - 3.4 oz (95 g)
  Syrup:
- Fresh lemon juice - 1/3 cup (80 ml)
- Powdered sugar - 2 cups (240 g)
- Water - 2 tbsp
- Butter, melted - 2 tbsp

Cook time: 35 minutes
Serves: 12

Per Serving:
Calories 422, Carbs 55g, Fat 20.64g, Protein 4.2g

DESSERT

Banana Bread

DIRECTIONS:

1. In a bowl, mix flour, sugar, baking soda, baking powder, and salt.
2. In a separate bowl, whisk eggs with butter, vanilla, and bananas until well blended.
3. Add flour mixture into the egg mixture and mix until well combined.
4. Pour batter into the greased air fryer loaf pan.
5. Place pan in air fryer basket and **Bake** for 35 minutes at 325 F/ 160 C.
6. Slice and serve.

INGREDIENTS:

- Eggs, lightly beaten - 2
- All-purpose flour - 1 cup (120 g)
- Baking soda - 1/4 tsp
- Baking powder - 1/2 tsp
- Sugar - 1/3 cup (67 g)
- Vanilla - 1 tsp
- Butter, melted - 1/4 cup (56 g)
- Mashed banana - 1 cup (225 g)
- Salt - 1/4 tsp

Cook time: 35 minutes
Serves: 10

Per Serving:
Calories 161, Carbs 22g,
Fat 6g, Protein 3.52g

Donuts

DIRECTIONS:

1. In a bowl, mix pancake mix, sugar, eggs, cinnamon, and oil until well combined.
2. Pour the donut mixture into the silicone donut molds.
3. Place donut molds into the air fryer basket and **Air Fry** at 350 F/ 175 C for 9 minutes.
4. Serve and enjoy.

INGREDIENTS:

- Eggs - 2
- Pancake mix - 2 cups (240 g)
- Vegetable oil - 1/2 cup (120 ml)
- Cinnamon - 1 1/2 tbsp
- Sugar - 1/4 cup (50 g)

Cook time: 9 minutes
Serves: 8

Per Serving:
Calories 286, Carbs 29g,
Fat 16g, Protein 6.78g

Carrot Cake

DIRECTIONS:

1. In a bowl, mix flour, baking powder, baking soda, salt, and cinnamon.
2. In a separate bowl, whisk eggs with oil, milk, and sugar.
3. Pour the egg mixture into the flour mixture and mix until well combined. Add grated carrots and fold well.
4. Pour batter into the air fryer-greased baking pan.
5. Place baking pan into the air fryer basket and **Bake** for 30-35 minutes at 320 F/ 160 C.
6. Slice and serve.

INGREDIENTS:

- Eggs, lightly beaten - 2
- Carrots, grated - 1 1/2 cups (150 g)
- All-purpose flour - 1 1/2 cups (180 g)
- Baking soda - 1/2 tsp
- Milk - 1/4 cup (60 ml)
- Cinnamon - 1 tsp
- Olive oil - 1/2 cup (120 ml)
- Brown sugar - 1 cup (200 g)
- Baking powder - 1 tsp
- Salt - 1/2 tsp

Cook time: 35 minutes
Serves: 10

Per Serving:
Calories 285, Carbs 38g,
Fat 13g, Protein 4.11g

Peanut Butter Cookies

DIRECTIONS:

1. In a bowl, mix peanut butter, vanilla, egg, and Swerve until smooth.
2. Make cookies from the peanut butter mixture, place them into the air fryer basket, and **Air Fry** at 320 F/ 160 C for 8 minutes.
3. Turn cookies and air fry for 6 minutes more.
4. Serve and enjoy.

INGREDIENTS:

- Egg - 1
- Peanut butter - 1 cup (240 g)
- Vanilla - 1 tsp
- Swerve - 1/3 cup (65 g)

Cook time: 14 minutes
Serves: 8

Per Serving:
Calories 110, Carbs 8g,
Fat 6.97g, Protein 3.39g

Pineapple Upside-Down Cake

DIRECTIONS:

1. Lightly grease the baking pan with cooking spray and set aside.
2. Add melted butter to the baking pan.
3. Make cake mix according to the packet instructions.
4. Place the pineapple slices in the prepared baking pan, then put the cherries in the middle and sprinkle them with brown sugar. Pour cake mix over it.
5. Place the cake pan in the air fryer basket and **Bake** for 20 minutes at 350 F/ 175 C
6. Let it cool completely.
7. Slice and serve.

INGREDIENTS:

- Cake mix - 1 box (450 g)
- Cherries - 4
- Brown sugar - 1/4 cup (55 g)
- Pineapple slices - 20 oz (565 g)
- Butter, melted - 2 tbsp

Cook time: 20 minutes
Serves: 8

Per Serving:
Calories 282, Carbs 62g,
Fat 3g, Protein 3.62g

Bread Pudding

DIRECTIONS:

1. Add bread cubes into the greased baking pan and sprinkle with chocolate chips.
2. In a bowl, mix heavy cream, vanilla, and sugar and pour over bread cubes.
3. Place baking pan into the air fryer basket and **Air Fry** at 350 F/ 175 C for 15 minutes.
4. Serve and enjoy.

INGREDIENTS:

- Egg - 1
- Bread cubes - 2 cups (180 g)
- Chocolate chips - 1/4 cup (45 g)
- Sugar - 1/4 cup (50 g)
- Vanilla - 1/2 tsp
- Heavy cream - 2/3 cup (160 ml)

Cook time: 15 minutes
Serves: 6

Per Serving:
Calories 116, Carbs 10g, Fat 6.95g, Protein 2.8g

This page is for your notes

Printed in Great Britain
by Amazon